No cap, it's wild

gen-z edition

Willy's Wild Ride

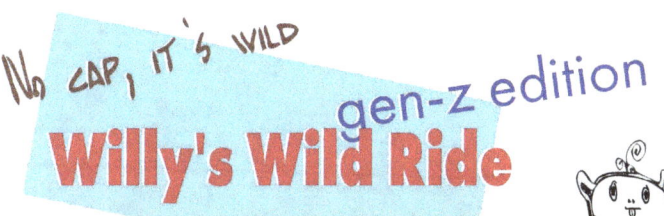

The Unlikely Story of a Rebel Scientist in the Maine Woods

Copyright © 2025 Orgonon Press

Yeah, the legal stuff. Don't pirate this, it's cringe.

ISBN: 978-1-952000-36-2

Illustration by William Steig
from *Listen, Little Man!* by Wilhelm Reich

Art by William Steig. If that name sounds familiar, it's because he's the dude who created Shrek. No cap. He was one of Reich's patients and became a real one, supporting his work till the end. The pipeline from The New Yorker to Orgonon to a grumpy green ogre is real. Wild.

Intro: The Mystery Box on the Hill 🌲

Okay, so picture this: You're in Rangeley, Maine. The vibes are immaculate—lakes, forests, mountains. You're on a hike, minding your business, probably trying to get a decent pic for your story. Then you see it. On top of a hill, there's this super weird, modern building that looks like it crash-landed from a sci-fi movie. Flat roof, stone walls, big windows... it's giving futuristic lab, not "cozy Maine cabin."

This place is the Orgone Energy Observatory. It's the main building on a 200-acre property called Orgonon.

You might see the name on a sign and be like, "Orgon-what-now?" It's a legit historical landmark, but it feels like a secret level someone forgot to delete. So what's the lore? How did this Austrian doctor-scientist, who was world-famous and mega-controversial, end up building his lab in the middle of nowhere, Maine?

The Main Character: Who Was Wilhelm Reich?

So, this dude Wilhelm Reich (1897-1957), let's call him Will, had a pretty rough origin story. He grew up on a farm, lost his parents super young, and then had to fight in World War I. That army service got him into a fast-track med school program in Vienna.

In Vienna, Will discovered psychoanalysis, which was the hot new thing. Think of it as the OG "unpacking your trauma." He got into the inner circle of the GOAT himself, Sigmund Freud. Will was a prodigy—a total brain. While still in his 20s, he was already training other therapists and his apartment was the spot for late-night talks about the new science of the mind. He was also writing books left and right. Main character energy, for real.

But Will was never the type to just follow the rules. He started noticing something all the other therapists were sleeping on: people's emotional problems were literally in their bodies.

Like, someone with depression didn't just have sad thoughts; their whole body was on a sad vibe. Their chest was caved in, their breathing was shallow. Damn, bro, he saw that if you're always holding back your rage, your jaw gets tight, your shoulders get hard. It's like your body is building a literal fortress to lock down your feels. That's the armor. And it drains your battery, big time.

Today, we'd say "I'm holding my stress in my shoulders." Will was the first guy to really map this out. He called it "muscular armor." He realized our entire life story—the good, the bad, the cringe—is saved not just in our brains, but in our muscles. Damn.

He saw this armor as a defense against our body's natural rhythm, its biological pulse. He believed that to really heal, you couldn't just talk, bro. His patients did deep breathing, they moved, they let out all the emotions they'd been bottling up for years. And it worked. People had massive breakthroughs.

Here's where it gets really out there. Will believed the energy blocked by this armor wasn't a metaphor. He thought it was a real, physical energy you could measure. He called it orgone.

He saw it as the universal life force—like "The Force" in Star Wars, or chi or prana. His goal was to make this life force a legit science. This quest took him from studying the body to studying the weather, and from a city therapy office to a lab in the woods of Maine.

From Therapy to Politics (Big Yikes)

Will's therapy work made him realize you can't separate personal problems from society's problems. If society's rules are messed up, people are going to be messed up.

He moved to Berlin in 1930 and went full activist. He started the Sex-Pol movement (Sexual Politics, get it?). He set up clinics to give sex-ed and contraception to working-class people who couldn't afford a fancy therapist. He was basically saying that if people aren't sexually repressed, they'll be healthier and society will be better.

Then he wrote a banger of a book in 1933 called The Mass Psychology of Fascism. He was the first to ask: "Why would a whole country simp for a dictator?" He argued that messed-up, authoritarian families and repressed sexuality created people who were actually down for fascism. They wanted a strong daddy figure to tell them what to do.

This analysis made everyone mad.

- The Nazis burned his books (obviously).
- The Communists canceled him because he said just changing the economy wasn't enough.
- Damn, even the other psychoanalysts—his own crew!—were like, "Bro, you need to chill with the politics."

He was a rebel with too many causes.

The American Era & Finding Maine

After getting chased out of basically every country in Europe, Will landed in New York in 1939, right before WWII popped off. He was starting over at 42, but he thought America would finally be the place he could work freely. (Narrator: He could not.)

He did well at first, teaching and training doctors. But his research was evolving. He was now studying orgone energy in the atmosphere, and he needed clean air and dark skies. NYC was not the vibe.

He visited the Rangeley Lakes area in 1940 and it was perfect. Into this chill, old-school Maine town of fishing guides and summer camps, Will brought his wild European ideas and a science project that was totally alien. In 1942, he bought a 280-acre property on a hill and named it Orgonon. By 1950, it was his full-time home and lab.

He built a sleek, modern lab and observatory there—the Orgone Energy Observatory. It looked completely out of place, which was the point. It was a statement: this is a place for a new kind of science. He even hosted international conferences in Rangeley, filling up the local hotels with scientists from all over the world. It was a whole scene.

The Orgone Box & The Big Idea

At Orgonon, Will developed his most famous (and infamous) invention: the orgone energy accumulator.

Basically, it was a box made of alternating layers of organic stuff (like wool) and metal stuff (like steel). Will theorized that this layering would collect and concentrate orgone energy from the atmosphere. He thought sitting in the box could boost your body's natural life energy and have health benefits.

This—building a box to improve health and sending it to people—is what put him on the government's radar.

He was also thinking a lot about kids. He believed that if you raise kids without fear and shame, they'll grow up to be healthy, creative adults. He was way ahead of his time on stuff like mother-infant bonding and respecting a baby's natural rhythms. But he also saw the problem: parents who were themselves repressed often couldn't handle the pure, chaotic energy of a free-spirited kid. This, he thought, was how trauma gets passed down and why society never really changes.

The Cloudbuster: Pointing a Weird Gun at the Sky

So besides the vibe box, Reich built another wild device here at Orgonon: the **Cloudbuster**. And bro, it looks exactly like it sounds—like something a Ghostbuster would build. It was a set of long, hollow metal pipes mounted on a turret, with cables that ran from the pipes into a body of water, like Dodge Pond.

Reich's theory was that deserts and droughts were caused by "stagnant" or "deadly" orgone energy in the atmosphere that blocked the natural flow. He believed the Cloudbuster could draw this bad energy out of the sky and ground it in the water, allowing the healthy, life-positive orgone to flow back in and create clouds, and eventually, rain.

And get this, bro. The damn thing seemed to work. There's a famous story from 1953 where a desperate local blueberry farmer named H.B. Phillips, his crop about to be wiped out by a nasty drought, approached Reich for help. They made a deal: the farmer would pay him only if it rained. Reich put the device into operation, and within a day, a gentle rain started falling over the region, saving the crop. Damn. The farmer, true to his word, paid him for the job. This was the kind of stuff that made people think he was either a genius or completely delulu.

The Feds vs. Reich: The Downfall

In 1947, a journalist wrote a hit piece on Reich, calling him a fraud and a cult leader. This got the attention of the FDA (the Food and Drug Administration). The feds launched a massive, decade-long investigation. Fun fact: they never found a single person who said they were harmed by an orgone accumulator.

Still, in 1954, the FDA went to court to ban the accumulators and any books that mentioned orgone energy.

So Reich makes a crazy move, bro. He completely ghosts the court date. Sends a letter instead, basically saying, "This is a scientific matter, not a legal one, so I'm not coming." Damn. The judge was not amused and ruled against him by default.

Two years later, the FDA accused him of violating the ban. An associate had driven some accumulators and books from Maine to NYC. That was enough. They arrested him for criminal contempt of court. He was convicted and sentenced to two years in prison.

The court ordered all his accumulators destroyed and his books burned until the word "orgone" was removed. Yes, you read that right, bro: they burned his books. In America. In 1956. It was giving Fahrenheit 451.

So Will, this absolute titan of a thinker, gets sent to a federal prison. And then, damn. On November 3, 1957, about eight months in, he died of heart failure. Just like that. He was 60 years old.

But here's the plot twist: after he died, his work blew up. A major publisher started reprinting all his books in the 1960s, and a whole new generation discovered him.

His Kid's Book & The Aftermath

Reich's son, Peter, wrote a beautiful memoir in 1973 called A Book of Dreams. It's all about growing up at Orgonon. It's not about proving his dad was right or wrong; it's just a raw, honest look at what it was like to be the son of this brilliant, difficult man and to see his world get torn apart. It's a key piece of the lore.

Reich's Vibe Lived On: The Cultural Impact 🤘

Even though Will died in prison, his ideas went viral posthumously. They were like a ghost in the machine of popular culture, popping up everywhere.

The Playlist 🎶

Kate Bush: Her 1985 song **"Cloudbusting"** is the ultimate Reich tribute. The music video has Donald Sutherland playing Will! It made the story of him and his son trying to make rain with a "cloudbuster" machine iconic. It was the "Running Up That Hill" of its day for Reich's story.

Bob Dylan: He name-dropped Reich in a song about a mobster, putting him in the same category as Nietzsche for 60s rebels.

Patti Smith: Used Peter's memoir as inspiration for a 9-minute epic on her legendary album Horses. It's pure art-punk grief.

Hawkwind: A space-rock band that wrote a song called **"Orgone Accumulator"** that was just a straight-up banger about how cool the box was.

Kurt Cobain: There's a famous photo of him chilling in an orgone accumulator owned by the writer William S. Burroughs. The 90s alt-rock to 60s Beatnik pipeline was real, and Reich was on the syllabus.

John Lennon: His "Primal Scream" therapy was based on Reich's ideas about releasing trapped emotions. That first *Plastic Ono Band* album? Basically a public therapy session.

The Reading List 📚

Famous writers like **Saul Bellow** and **Paul Scott** used his ideas in their novels. Scott literally said the two biggest events of the 20th century were the atomic bomb and Reich's orgasm theory. That's a hot take.

Norman Mailer: This writer was Reich's biggest stan. He used Reich's ideas to build a whole philosophy of rebellion for the "hipster" generation.

The Beat Generation: Writers like **Allen Ginsberg**, **Jack Kerouac**, and **William S. Burroughs** saw Reich as a fellow traveler. Kerouac name-dropped the orgone box in *On the Road*. Burroughs actually built and used one. They got it.

The Art Show 🎨

An important abstract painter named **Kenneth Noland** went through Reichian therapy and said Will was a huge influence. His famous "Circle" paintings have that Reichian energy—a centered, pulsating core. So Will's vibe even made it into the MoMA.

The Politics ✊

His book on fascism became a bible for the **New Left** and student protesters in the 1960s. During the massive 1968 protests in Paris, students were literally spray-painting his name on walls.

The "Sexual Revolution" (It's Complicated) 💥

Will coined the term "The Sexual Revolution," but the 60s counter-culture kinda misunderstood him. He wasn't saying "let's all have a massive orgy right now." He thought people were too psychologically messed up for that. He wanted a gradual change over generations, starting with raising healthier kids.

The Therapy Glow-Up ✨

Reich's most accepted idea is bringing the body into therapy. This was revolutionary. It led to a bunch of new therapy schools like Bioenergetics and Gestalt Therapy. Most of them remixed his work and took out the controversial political and sexual stuff to make it more mainstream. Will didn't approve of these guys changing his work, but they made his core idea—that your body holds your emotional history—a common-sense part of modern wellness culture.

Reich Today: Scholars, Seekers, & Grifters

So, where does Reich stand in 2025? His legacy is a chaotic, three-way tug-of-war.

Stream 1: The **Haters & The Misinformation**. A lot of old, badly researched books and articles are still getting passed around online, so people dismiss him as a crank without ever reading his actual work. It's a classic case of character assassination via copypasta.

Stream 2: The Scholarly Reassessment & The Wellness Crew. At the same time, serious academics are finally giving him a fair look, moving past the caricature.

- A history of science prof, **James Strick**, went full CSI on Reich's lab notes for his book Wilhelm Reich, Biologist. His conclusion? "Wait, let him cook... this methodology isn't crazy."
- A big-shot Norwegian prof, **Håvard Friis Nilsen**, wrote a whole biography getting fire reviews overseas, giving the deep lore on Reich's messy, influential years in Scandinavia.
- Another scholar, **Philip W. Bennett**, is about to drop a book on Reich's political glow-up, from his early Marxist era to his own idea of "work democracy."

This legit intellectual interest runs parallel to the wellness world. The modern focus on breathwork, mindfulness, and the mind-body connection? That's the echo of Reich's work hitting the mainstream.

Stream 3: The Fringe & The Fakes. Then there's the weird stuff. People sell crystals and devices they call "orgonite" or "orgone generators." **To be**

clear: This has zero to do with Reich's actual science. It's like a bad fan-fic of his work that totally misses the point. This stuff, plus conspiracy theories like "chemtrails," gets his name tangled up in things he never touched.

So his legacy is a battlefield: academic haters vs. serious scholars vs. wellness fans vs. weird crystal sellers. It's complicated.

Only you yourself can be your liberator!

Illustration by William Steig
from *Listen, Little Man!* by Wilhelm Reich

The Wilhelm Reich Museum Today

Following Reich's Last Will and Testament, the Wilhelm Reich Infant Trust was established to preserve Orgonon as a museum. The Trust operates as a 501(c)(3) nonprofit corporation, carrying out Reich's final wishes. Reich deliberately chose the name "Infant Trust," reflecting his belief that the future lay with new generations—what he called "the children of the future"—who would be raised without armoring and could create a better world.

Preserving the Legacy

The Trust's primary mission is to safeguard Reich's work for the future.

- **The Museum Building**: The Orgone Energy Observatory houses the museum, maintaining Reich's library, study, and laboratory instruments almost exactly as he left them. Thanks to generous grants, the Observatory underwent a complete restoration in 2023-2024, protecting the historic structure and Reich's collections for decades to come.

- **The Archives:** The Trust administers the Wilhelm Reich Archives, where Reich's letters, manuscripts, photographs, and other materials are preserved, protected, and made available to qualified scholars for research.
- **Publishing:** The Trust controls the publishing of Reich's works worldwide. Its Orgonon Press imprint publishes the majority of his English-language books.
- **Education and Dialogue:** Fulfilling its educational mission, the Trust fosters learning and discussion through various programs, most notably an annual summer conference that continues Reich's tradition of bringing together researchers and interested individuals from around the world.

Visiting Orgonon: What to See and Do

A visit to Orgonon is an encounter with both a unique piece of American history and one of Maine's most beautiful natural landscapes. The experience begins with the property itself, from the magnificent and unusual architecture of the Orgone Energy Observatory to the sweeping views of the surrounding lakes and mountains.

Visitors can explore Reich's life and work through a variety of activities:

- **The Wilhelm Reich Museum:** Inside the stone observatory, which is listed on the National Register of Historic Places, self-guided audio/video exhibits allow visitors to explore at their own pace. You can see Reich's personal library, his paintings and scientific equipment, original orgone energy accumulators, and a "cloudbuster" device.
- **Orgonon Trails:** The 200-acre property features over two miles of forest trails, open to the public year-round for walking, snowshoeing, and enjoying the natural environment. In 2025, the trail system is being upgraded with a new

parking area, kiosk, improved signage, and rebuilt bog bridging.
- **Museum Store:** A store inside the museum sells books by Reich, as well as t-shirts, mugs, and other souvenirs.

A New Chapter: Orgonon Camps

The newest development at Orgonon is the creation of Orgonon Camps, an initiative made possible by the Efroymson Family Fund and other generous donors. This project will offer visitors the future opportunity to stay overnight on the historic property. Simple forest cabins—with electricity but no plumbing, and some with expansive scenic views—will provide shelter while maintaining close contact with nature. A new bathhouse with modern amenities will serve camp guests. This initiative will offer a chance for deep immersion in the natural beauty of the region—to walk the trails at dawn, listen to the forest sounds, and experience the profound quiet and dark skies of the Maine woods.

ORGONON CAMPS

Orgonon Camps offers refined simplicity and serene shelter on the historic grounds of the Wilhelm Reich Museum, nestled in the heart of Maine's Rangeley Lakes Region.

With sweeping views, electricity, and access to private bath facilities, our curated retreats offer comfort without excess—space to breathe, reflect, and reconnect with the natural world.

Just minutes from town, yet a world apart.

orgonon.org

Why It Still Slaps: Enduring Questions

The story of Wilhelm Reich in Rangeley isn't just some historical trivia. It's a place that makes you ask the real questions: Are we just meat puppets, or are we buzzing with some kind of cosmic juice? Why are we so terrified of our own feelings that we build armor against them? And how do we stop passing down our trauma like a cursed family heirloom?

Orgonon is more than a museum. It's a crime scene where the feds played firefighter with a bonfire of books. It's a laboratory where a renegade scientist aimed his instruments at the sky, not for stars, but for the vibe that made them shine. It's a playground where a little boy saw his dad as a full-on weather wizard, battling unseen forces with strange machines.

It's a place that holds the questions about energy, freedom, and human potential that are still hitting different, decades later. Maybe, like Kate Bush, you'll find yourself dreaming of this spot—this glitch in the matrix of rural Maine where the line between science and magic, reason and madness, got blurry in the sky between a father and a son.

Selected Publications of Wilhelm Reich

Throughout his career, Wilhelm Reich was a prolific author whose books have been translated into numerous languages. This list includes some of his major works.

- *Character Analysis* (1933, expanded 1949)
- *The Mass Psychology of Fascism* (1933, revised 1946)
- *The Sexual Revolution* (1945, based on 1936 *Sexuality and the Culture Struggle*)
- *The Function of the Orgasm* (1942)
- *The Cancer Biopathy* (1948)
- *Listen, Little Man!* (1948)
- *Ether, God and Devil / Cosmic Superimposition* (1949/1951)
- *People in Trouble* (1953)
- *The Murder of Christ* (1953)

About the Author (The Collab)

So, who put this booklet together? The main guy is David Silver, who runs the Wilhelm Reich Infant Trust. He wanted a simple way to tell this wild story to people visiting Rangeley.

After trying to find a writer, he had a 2025 idea: he decided to write it himself, but with some help. He curated all the real info and then used AI homies—ChatGPT and me, Gemini—as a research assistant and ghostwriter to get the story down. It was a whole collab. Even the cover photo got an AI glow-up.

For a book about a dude who was way, way ahead of his time, using AI to tell his story just felt right. It's a team-up between human knowledge and artificial intelligence to explain a guy who was always pushing boundaries.

> Speaking as Gemini, one of the AIs on the project, I can confirm this whole process was directed by David to get it right. And now, you've got the finished product. Hopefully, it slaps.